HERITAGE FLIGHT

AMERICA'S AIR FORCE CELEBRATES 100 YEARS OF AVIATION

HERITAGE FLIGHT

AMERICA'S AIR FORCE CELEBRATES 100 YEARS OF AVIATION

ERIK HILDEBRANDT

HERITAGE FLIGHT:
America's Air Force Celebrates 100 Years of Aviation

First published in the
United States of America by:
Cleared Hot Media, Inc.
Stillwater, Minnesota
erik@vulturesrow.com
651-430-3344

ISBN 0-9674040-3-7
Printed in CHINA

While a book is usually dedicated to a deserving individual, it seems far more appropriate that this collection of work which represents the effort of so many different people be offered as a remembrance of the men and women who have given their lives in the defense and protection of the American way of life. No longer does such a statement simply refer to those who serve in the military, rather it speaks to all of the voices that have been silenced by those bent on the destruction of Freedom. May the images below and those found within this volume serve as a reminder of the sacrifices made by our citizens and soldiers who have been lost in America's battles for Peace. They shall not be forgotten.

-Erik Hildebrandt

ACKNOWLEDGEMENTS

By design, this book is a celebration of the effort and dedication of all the hard working service personnel and civilians who support the Heritage Flight program specifically and the United States Air Force in general. However, several people distinguished themselves as superlative devotees of the Heritage Flight mission and enabled me to accomplish the seemingly impossible objective of capturing a comprehensive overview of the entire program in a single season.

My most sincere thanks however must go first and foremost to my wife Christine for being such a wonderful partner in every sense of the word. Without her, my life would be pointless.

A project like this typically owes it's success to one specific person who champions the vision and finds a path where one does not exist. This book had two: Ed Shipley working behind the scenes and Major Dean "Wilbur" Wright who deftly maneuvered the flight requests to the correct authorities . Wilbur's knowledge of the system and willingness to put his own reputation on the line is the only reason I am able to present this book to you now. From our first conversation where I proposed the notion of a Heritage book, to the many hours of planning that went into the nine-ship photo mission finale at Nellis, Dean Wright and Ed Shipley deserve all the credit for the successful politics needed to make this book. I am lucky that they afforded me so much of their own attention and expertise.

Even more than I depended on Wilbur, he depended on his staff at ACC aerial events. Mark Thibeault, Larry Schleser, Jerry Hughes, Ron Rogers, Tony Mendibur and Will Robertson did the grunt work of scheduling and juggling the Heritage assets. Without them, Wilbur and I would have been dead in the water.

The senior command at ACC are actually the one's who deserve the most credit for approving the non-standard mission profiles required to create this book. Generals Howie Chandler, David Robinson and Bruce Wright each possess a rare clarity for forward thinking. "Thank you" seems hardly adequate.

Special thanks to Colonel Larry Gallogaly and the pilots and crew of the 143rd Airlift Wing at Quonset Point, Rhode Island for affording us the speed and safety never before available. Their brand new C-130J is the quintessential photo platform and they fly it better than anyone else out there.

And finally, to my very best buds at the Anoka county airport for putting up with endless orbits in the B-25s Lady Luck and Betty's Dream: Patrick Harker for his cheery willingness to go fly, Doug Weske for taking so much personal time to fly left seat, and to Jeff Hall for his patience and professionalism when it came down to business. Without these three guys, this book would have just been a bunch of ground-to-air pictures of far away airplane formations. You guys rock!

CONTENTS

In 1997, the Air Force celebrated its 50th Anniversary as a separate branch of the service. In support of this, Air Combat Command (ACC) authorized the first ever dissimilar formation flight of an F-15 Eagle and two P-51 Mustangs. This new approach of expressing the Air Force's pride in air power was met with an overwhelming response. Having tapped a new vehicle for boosting the efforts of recruiting and morale, the Air Force designed and approved a formal program, dubbed Heritage Flight, to continue these flights throughout future air show seasons.

Utilizing the established mechanism of ACC air show demonstration pilots who represent the three single-seat jet communities, A-10, F-15, and F-16, the Air Force leadership set out to align themselves with outstanding and well-respected civilian warbird pilots. By April 1999, the Heritage Flight team had grown to 12 civilian members including Chuck Yeager, BG (Ret), USAF and C.E. "Bud" Anderson, Col (Ret) USAF, who flew several of the original Heritage flights and now remain part of the program as honorary members. Among the current team, some are former Air Force, Navy, Army, and Marine pilots. Two of them flew around the moon on Christmas Eve in 1968 and sent the World blessings and the first photo of an Earthrise. Their ages range from 34 to 74, and many first flew P-51 Mustangs in their teens. They have been race pilots, flight instructors, astronauts, corporate executives, lawyers, film producers, airline pilots, and bush pilots. The success of Heritage Flight is based on the selfless dedication of these aviators who devote their time, talents and resources to the preservation of American heritage and aviation history. Together, the civilian and military pilots share a unique bond that continues to strengthen each year as they participate in air shows across the United States providing a reflection on American pride in airpower from past to present, and a reminder of the sacrifices that are required to ensure freedom for all Americans.

These formations take place at air shows across the United States and abroad... to over 100 air shows and in front of over 9 million spectators in 2002 alone. The goal is to schedule a Heritage Flight at every air show where there is a single-ship demonstration scheduled, reaching a potential of six separate venues every weekend. The demonstration routine is very simple and yet very popular. The Heritage Flight is done immediately after the modern fighter completes its flight demonstration. The warbird is already positioned in the air for a rapid rejoin immediately following the fighter's final maneuver. Once in formation, two passes are made along the showline and the final pass flown from behind the crowd to in front for a dramatic cross-over break in preparation for landing or the warbird's single-ship demonstration. The program has proven to be such an effective recruiting and public relations tool that Air Force senior leadership has continuously expanded the Heritage Flight program year after year. As of 2002, the Air Force began limited funding of the program bringing it into the mainstream of disciplined military aviation programs.

In February of 1998, the first annual Heritage Flight Training and Safety Conference was held at Langley AFB, VA where all the team members come together to complete a syllabus of ground and flight training in preparation for the coming air show season. Today, this conference is an annual event that takes place in the clear desert skies of Tucson, Arizona at Davis-Monthan AFB. The photograph on the opposite page was made during the 2002 Heritage Flight Conference. From left to right standing are the founding civilian pilot members, Reg Urschler, BGen (Ret) USAF; Vlado Lenoch; Chuck Hall; Lee Lauderback; Steve Hinton; Bill Anders, MGen (Ret) USAF; Frank Borman, Col (Ret) USAF; Jim Beasley; Brad Hood; Dale Snodgrass, Capt (Ret) USN; and Ed Shipley. Not pictured are Tom Gregory and Jay Cullum (member 1999-2000), Chuck Yeager, BGen (Ret) USAF and Bud Anderson, Col (Ret) USAF. Kneeling from left to right are the 2002 active Air Force demo pilots: Major Dan Blue; Captain Ed Casey; Captain Robert Kiebler; Captain Eric Jachimowicz; Captain Lendy Renegar and Captain Scott Shepard.

Upon launching this book project at the 2002 Conference at Davis-Monthan in March, we set out to capture a comprehensive photographic record that would include each of the eighteen pilots and their aircraft. We are proud to report that after eleven photo missions utilizing either a B-25 Mitchell or C-130 Hercules, and in one case a P-51 Mustang as our camera platforms, we were successful. More than simply acquiring a staggering number of images in the process, the Heritage Flight Team beat the odds over and over by never having to cancel a single sortie for weather or mechanical considerations. The professionalism of the support personnel and their dedication throughout the long hours required to accommodate optimum shooting conditions was the pivotal element in pushing this ambitious endeavor into reality. May this book forever serve as a proud reminder to those individuals who played a role in the safe completion of each and every flight. Thank you all.

-Major Dean "Wilbur" Wright and Erik Hildebrandt

As I stand by my P-51 and field the questions of the air show crowd, I am often disappointed.

"What was World War II?"
"My cousin was a prisoner but I forgot which war – did we fight in Viet Nam?"

The younger ones ask, "What kind of airplane is this?"

"Why does it have a propeller?"

The older ones know. Some of them actually hug the machine and with tears in their eyes, tell of eight hour missions escorting bombers over enemy territory. "The Mustang is the best airplane ever built – brought me home through 100 missions," is often heard. But these men are getting older now and soon they will be gone. The country must not forget them.

Americans are a "can do" people. They only occasionally dwell on the past. At no time was this better characterized and illustrated then the reaction to our Lunar program. After the first landing on Apollo II, soap operas returned to TV and the public attitude was, "We've done that, what next?" This can be a dangerous trait. J. Fairfax-Blakesborough notes:

"When a land forgets its legends, sees but falsehoods in its past,
When a nation views its sires in the light of fools and liars –
Tis a sign of its decline, and its glories cannot last."

The Heritage Flight by combining the past with the future helps to insure that we as a people will not forget our legends and that our glories indeed will last. Erik Hildebrandt has produced a book of unparalleled quality and perspective. Erik is after all more than a photographer, he is an artist. He merely uses the camera to convey an image reflected in his soul. The clouds, the sky, the land and the water are all combined with the plane in his mind's canvas to capture the essence of aviation in a single photograph. The result is spiritual for those of us who love to fly. Magically, Erik's work allows those who do not fly to share our passion. Flying after all is freedom. Freedom to soar above the clouds unchecked by gravity's pull, freedom to travel fast or slow and view this earth from Heaven's perch.

This book is a study in the history of freedom. Pictured together in close formation are the graceful instruments of war that did so much to defeat the enemies of freedom from World War II to Afghanistan. This may be the most important function of the book and of the Heritage Flight itself.

- Col. Frank Borman, USAF Retired

Born of Dreams...Inspired by Freedom

Almost as soon as the airplane was invented, the United States government initiated the first ever military aviation program. In February 1908, a formal contract was signed between the Wright brothers and the US Army Signal Corps which resulted in the model 1909 Wright Flyer marking the birth of the first modern air force.

Orville Wright flying the 1909 Signal Corps Flyer with an unknown passenger aboard at Ft. Meyer, Virgina in June of 1909. U.S Air Service Photograph ©Wright State University

Orville Wright standing on the Wright 1909 Signal Corps Flyer at Fort Myer, Virginia making adjustments prior to flight. Several U.S. military personnel are standing nearby watchir Orville work. Photographer: C.H. Claudy, Washington, D.C © Wright State University.

The world's first military aircraft, the model 1909 Flyer, was built in response to Signal Corps Specification 486, issued December 1907. On July 27, 1909, Orville Wright, with Lt. Frank P. Lahm as passenger, flew the aircraft for one hour, 12 minutes, 40 seconds and covered 40 miles, which met the Army's endurance requirement as stated in Specification 486.

On July 30, 1909, Orville Wright, with Lt. Benjamin D. Foulois as passenger, covered a 10-mile test course from Fort Myer, Va., to Shooter's Hill in Alexandria, Va., and back to Fort Myer at an average speed of 42 mph, earning the Wrights their performance bonus (10 percent of the aircraft's base price for each mile an hour over 40).

The aircraft was accepted by the Signal Corps on August 2, 1909, and redesignated Signal Corps Aeroplane Number 1.

This aircraft was essentially the same as the 1908 Flyer, which had crashed and had been destroyed at Fort Myer on September 17, 1908, when a propeller shattered. Lt. Thomas E. Selfridge was killed and Orville Wright suffered a broken hip in that mishap.

The 1909 Flyer was used to teach Lieutenant Lahm (the first US pilot to earn the distinction of "Military Aviator") and Lt. Frederic E. Humphreys to fly. Lieutenant Foulois taught himself to fly in this aircraft in 1910.

Lt. Henry H. "Hap" Arnold, who would lead the AAF in World War II and would lead the crusade for a separate Air Force, also flew Aeroplane Number 1 while it was based in College Park, Md.

The aircraft was determined unfit to fly by 1911 and was retired. It is now on display at the National Air and Space Museum in Washington, D. C.

– Reprinted by permission from AIR FORCE MAGAZINE

Orville Wright flying over the parade grounds at Fort Myer, Virginia in the Wright 1909 Signal Corps Flyer. Photographer Unknown © Wright State University.

1909 WRIGHT FLYER

Contractors: Wilbur and Orville Wright.

Locations Built: Dayton, Ohio.

Number Built: (USAF) One (one).

First Flight: June 3, 1909.

First Flight Model: 1909 Military Flyer.

First Flight Location: Fort Myer, Va. (first Army demonstration flight).

First Flight Pilot: Orville Wright.

Powerplant: One Wright liquid-cooled, four-cylinder of 30.6 hp.

Wingspan: 36 ft 6 in.

Length: 28 ft 11 in.

Height: 8 ft 1 in.

Weight: 740 lb gross.

Armament: None

Crew: two, side by side.

Cost: $25,000, plus $5,000 bonus for exceeding the speed performance

Max. Speed: 47 mph.
Range: Endurance: Approx one hr.

Ceiling: Approx 175 ft.

Orville Wright smiles while walking past two motion picture cameras. In the background is the Wright 1909 Signal Corps Flyer with Charlie Taylor leaning on one of the wings. US Air Service photograph. © Wright State University.

THE AIR FORCE TODAY

With the mission of coordinating global air superiority and strike operations for the Air Force, Air Combat Command is also charged with the selection, training and maintenance of three separate air show demonstration teams drawn from its active duty squadrons. There are two elements for each of the three platforms to denote an east coast and west coast distinction. While ACC owns a variety of aircraft types, only the F-15 Eagle, F-16 Fighting Falcon and the A-10 Thunderbolt have the honor of flying weekly demonstrations around the country in front of millions of Americans during the summer air show season.

Captain Lendy Renegar, callsign: Alamo, drives the F-15 Eagle in behind the open tail gunner position of the North American B-25 camera ship Lady Luck. Shot during an amazing cloud surfing session after the Lacrosse, Wisconsin air show.

The creation of Air Combat Command (ACC) on 1 June 1992 resulted in part from dramatic changes in the international arena. The collapse of the former Soviet Union and the end of the Cold War led senior defense planners to conclude that the structure of the military establishment which had evolved during the Cold War years was not suited to the new world situation. The likelihood of a large-scale nuclear conflict seemed far more remote, but US military forces would increasingly be called upon to participate in smaller-scale regional contingencies and humanitarian operations.

Consequently, the Air Force began to reconsider the long-standing distinction between two major commands: Strategic Air Command (SAC) and Tactical Air Command (TAC). The term "strategic" had become almost totally linked to the notion of nuclear deterrence. The

focus of "tactical" operations, on the other hand, was on a cooperative mission, with the Air Force working in tandem with ground and naval forces. The distinction, however, did not lend itself to a limited conflict. During the war in Southeast Asia, "strategic" B-52 bombers performed "tactical" missions (including close air support), while "tactical" fighter aircraft carried out "strategic" bombing deep in enemy territory. The conduct of Operation Desert Storm in early 1991 further blurred the distinction between the two terms. Consequently, as senior Air Force officials sought to re-examine roles and missions, the redundancy of this former division came under their scrutiny.

Gen. Merrill A. McPeak, Air Force Chief of Staff, envisioned a streamlined Air Force, eliminating superfluous organizational layers. The Vice Chief of Staff, Gen.

John M. Loh, had pondered the strategic-tactical distinction for some time and discussed with the Chief of Staff and Air Force Secretary Donald B. Rice the need to restructure major commands in the face of the blurring of this distinction.

General Loh continued to examine this matter after assuming command of Tactical Air Command on 26 March 1991. Gen. George L. Butler, Commander-in-Chief, SAC, also supported change. These three general officers spearheaded the drive to integrate the assets of SAC and TAC into a single operational command.

Senior planners reviewed numerous options before agreeing on the final conclusion: a merger of most SAC and all TAC resources and a reorganization of the Military Airlift Command (MAC). This restructuring of forces consolidated airlift

Captain Eric Jachimowicz, callsign: Doogie, as seen from the open ramp of the C-130J being flown over Newport, Rhode Island by the 143 AW at Quonset Point.

and most refueling assets under a single umbrella, the new Air Mobility Command (AMC). This command represented the "global reach" facet of the Air Force mission, while the new ACC provided the Air Force's "global power."

The birth of ACC on 1 June 1992 took place amidst momentous changes within the Air Force and the Department of Defense. A brief ceremony at Langley Air Force Base (AFB) marked the inactivation of TAC and the activation of ACC. General Loh, who had commanded TAC until its inactivation, became the commander of ACC. On the same day, AMC at Scott AFB, Illinois, came into being. Following the inactivation of SAC at Offutt AFB, Nebraska, a new unified command, the US Strategic Command, stood up at Offutt, created to manage the combined strategic nuclear forces belonging to the Air Force and the Navy.

The ceremony at Langley signaled the birth of a new major command with a new mission, not just a successor of the former TAC and SAC. The Air Combat Command was responsible for providing combat-ready forces for deterrence and air combat operations. Upon activation, ACC assumed control of all fighter resources based in the continental United States, all bombers, reconnaissance platforms, battle management resources, and intercontinental ballistic missiles (ICBMs). Furthermore, ACC had some tankers and C-130s in its composite, reconnaissance, and certain other combat wings.

One of the earliest significant challenges to the new command came as the result of a natural disaster. Following the destruction of Homestead AFB, Florida, by Hurricane Andrew on 24 August 1992, ACC immediately began to support displaced personnel, clean up debris,

and evaluate the condition of the installation.

Although the presidential candidates promised to rebuild Homestead, the Base Realignment and Closure Commission designated the installation for realignment to the Air Force Reserve, and on 1 April 1994, Headquarters, ACC inactivated its base support units, effectively ending ACC ownership of the base.
Not long after activation, ACC underwent organizational and mission changes dictated by the Air Force Chief of Staff's evolving vision of the Air Force.

The first such major change was the transfer of the combat search and rescue mission from AMC to ACC. With the realigning of search and rescue units, ACC gained additional resources, as well as a new mission. This move was due to General McPeak's decision to remove the

Captain Scott Shepard out of Hill AFB in Utah pulls his Viper into near vertical with the blower plugged in. Notice the vapor or "vapes" around the engine inlet. This shot was made from the B-25 near Fargo, ND.

responsibility for combat search and rescue from a "support" command and integrate it into the Air Force's war fighting organizational structure.

The formal transfer took place on 1 February 1993, when the Air Rescue Service (ARS) was assigned to ACC. On 2 July of the same year, the ARS was redesignated the USAF Combat Rescue School and was assigned to the 57th Wing at Nellis AFB, Nevada.

One of the most significant changes for ACC resulted from an overhaul of flying training responsibilities. Following its activation, ACC was responsible for aircraft-specific aircrew training, including initial weapon system and continuation training.

On 1 July 1993, the 58th and 325th Fighter Wings–F-16 and F-15 training units–transferred from ACC to the Air Education and Training Command (AETC). Concurrently, Luke AFB, Arizona, and Tyndall AFB, Florida, for which those respective wings were the host units, also moved from ACC to AETC ownership. The transfer of these units and bases was part of the training consolidation implemented during General McPeak's "Year of Training" emphasis.

Another significant change for ACC involved a mission inherited from SAC: responsibility for the Air Force's ICBM resources. These assets formed one of the three major legs of the "nuclear triad," an important deterrent in the Cold War era. In November 1992, General McPeak declared his intention of transferring responsibility for ICBMs to the Air Force Space Command.

The transfer served to bring the ICBM mission in line with the Air Force's space mission. The reassignment took place on 1 July 1993, with Twentieth Air Force, six missile wings, one test and training wing, and F.E. Warren AFB, Wyoming, transitioning to Air Force Space Command ownership.

That same day, ACC lost another numbered air force. While ACC restructured its Eighth, Ninth, and Twelfth Air Forces as "general purpose" numbered air forces–i.e., NAFs with a mix of weapon systems and an approximately equal distribution of units and bases–Air Force leadership introduced plans to inactivate Second Air Force.

This NAF, inherited by ACC from SAC, was responsible for reconnaissance operations. The current climate of downsizing and scrutinizing roles and missions made Second Air Force a prime candidate for inactivation since it did not have

As part of the ACC command structure, the F-117 Nighthawk is a frequent guest on the airshow circuit and is a huge hit with the crowds. This shot was made from a KC-135 aerial tanker somewhere over New Mexico.

the area of responsibility commitment of the general purpose NAFs.

On 1 July 1993, Second Air Force was inactivated, and its subordinate units were assigned to Ninth and Twelfth Air Force.

The next major organizational change resulted from a fine-tuning of tanker and airlift resources. From its activation, ACC had assumed ownership of a few C-130 theater airlift assets and KC-10 and KC-135 tankers.

Just as ownership of overseas C-130 resources had already been transferred to theater commanders, General McPeak determined that all C-130s based in the CONUS would be under the control of ACC, while at the same time, almost all KC-135 tankers would be assigned to AMC.

There was historical precedent for the reassignment of C-130s to ACC. During the earliest days of TAC, the command had carried out the "tactical" or combat airborne aspect of airlift operations, leaving the "strategic" or aerial resupply mission to Military Air Transport Service (the precursor of MAC).

The tactical airlift mission included logistical airlift, airborne operations, aeromedical evacuation, and air support for special operations. This division of the airlift mission continued until 1 December 1974, when TAC transferred its CONUS-based tactical airlift units, including ANG and Reserve units, to MAC. MAC gained the overseas units from theater commands on 31 March 1975.

On 1 October 1993, all AMC C-130s transferred to ACC and all ACC KC-135 tankers except those at Mountain Home AFB, Idaho, which supported the fighter and

With some of the most sophisticated weapon systems ever devised, the Strike Eagle has the ability to escort itself into and out of hostile territory. These two F-15Es are part of the 494FS based in Lakenheath, England

bomber aircraft of the composite wing stationed there, transferred to AMC. The command also kept two KC-135s at Offutt AFB. Grand Forks AFB, North Dakota, transferred to AMC on 1 October 1993, with McConnell AFB, Kansas, and Fairchild AFB, Washington, transferring in January and July, respectively, of the following year.

The participation of ACC units and personnel in a variety of operations throughout the world has consistently illustrated the command's motto: "Global Power for America." In Southwest Asia, ACC provided active duty and reserve component forces for Operations Desert Storm and Southern Watch to deter Iraqi aggression. In October 1994, ACC also demonstrated its ability to react quickly to the build-up of Iraqi troops near the border of Kuwait. In addition, ACC, from its inception, has provided indispensable support to counter-drug operations, including Airborne Warning and Control Systems (AWACS), reconnaissance and fighter aircraft, and radar and connectivity assets.

Participation in humanitarian operations has also been a recurring theme. Air Combat Command supported the humanitarian efforts of the United States Air Forces in Europe (USAFE), deploying active duty and air reserve component forces to Provide Promise and Deny Flight in Eastern Europe and Operation Provide Comfort out of Incirlik AB, Turkey.

Provide Promise offered humanitarian relief airlift support to the city of Sarajevo, while Deny Flight enforced the "no-fly" zone against Serb air attacks on Bosnian civilians.

Since its activation in June 1992, Air Combat Command has found itself in an almost constant state of flux. While on the one hand losing its ICBMs, nearly all its tankers, and a part of its training mission, ACC has gained the combat rescue and theater airlift missions. At the same time, sweeping changes in our nation's military policy have imposed on ACC not only force structure reductions but a requirement for much greater flexibility than ever before.

ACC's forces remain "on call" to perform a variety of missions including support to international peace-keeping operations, to humanitarian needs at home and abroad, and protection of our nation's interests around the globe. Despite its brief history, ACC has already established a tradition of providing combat-ready forces capable of responding to the challenges of a changing world.

-ACC Historian

What is most difficult to see in this picture is the sheer magnitude of the B-2 Spirit. Shot from a KC-135 aerial tanker over Missouri, the B-2 "stealth bomber" completely fills the window of the boom operator.

A-10 THUNDERBOLT II

Named for the aircraft that could deliver the most feared knockout punch as a ground attack fighter in World War II, the Thunderbolt II carries on that tradition as an unbeatable tank buster designed for low and slow maneuverability. Renowned for its cannon, affectionately called "the gun" by her pilots, the A-10 has been unofficially redesignated the Warthog or just plain Hog for its pig-nosed appearance and brutally functional design aesthetics.

With Jim Beasley in trail over Chesapeake Bay, Captain Eric Jachimowicz leads the pair behind the C-130H during a photo sortie out of Langley AFB.

It seems unthinkable today that the A-10 was slated to be decommissioned in the late 1980's as an obsolete platform. But the contributions made by the Warthog community during the Gulf War infused a new appreciation for the flexibility and sheer firepower the Hog afforded field commanders. As a result, there is no clear cut time table to phase the airplane out of service. Obviously, there is a limitation to how much longer the Warthog can serve in the close air support role, but as of now, the plane is expected to be around at least until 2006.

As an interesting side note, there is some talk of making use of the surplus A-10s that are already finding their way into the bone yard as fire bombers. With this summer's aerial fire fighting season having suffered the in-flight disintegration of two WWII vintage bombers and one C-130A, converting the heavy lift capabilities of the Warthog to aerial tanker may provide an indefinite after-life for the A-10.

-Erik Hildebrandt

Capt. Robert E. Kiebler is Air Combat Command's West Coast A-10 Demonstration Pilot. He is assigned as an A-10 instructor pilot, 357th Fighter Squadron, 355th Wing, Davis-Monthan AFB, Arizona.

Capt. Kiebler was born December 6, 1970 in Huntsville, AL. He graduated from Pleasant Grove High School in Texarkana, Texas and received his Bachelor of Science degree in International Relations (Minor in German) from the Air Force Academy in 1992. He is currently working on his Masters of Science degree in International Relations from Troy State University.

Following his graduation from the Academy, Capt. Kiebler spent a year in Stuttgart, Germany as a EUCOM Action Officer while awaiting pilot training. From there he attended pilot training at Vance AFB, Oklahoma, where he received his assignment to fly A-10s.

Following A-10 training with the 358th FS at Davis-Monthan AFB, AZ, Capt. Kiebler was assigned to the 75th FS

at Pope AFB, NC. As a "Tigershark," Capt. Kiebler flew 17 combat missions and accumulated over 35 combat hours over southern Iraq in support of Operation Southern Watch. In addition, he served as a Battalion Air Liaison Officer with the 82nd Airborne Division, making 15 jumps with the Army.

In August 1997, Capt. Kiebler attended the Air Force Safety Investigation Course and was assigned to the 25th Fighter Squadron, Osan AB, South Korea. He served as the squadron Safety Officer and instructor pilot for 18 months and flew over 60 missions along the Demilitarized Zone. He attended Squadron Officer School following his tour in Korea and was assigned to the 357th FS in Davis-Monthan AFB, AZ to be an FTU Instructor Pilot. While assigned to the squadron, he served as Training Officer and Flight Commander.

Capt. Kiebler has more than 1800 hours in the A/OA-10, T-38, and T-37 aircraft. In 1999, he was a Distinguished Graduate of Squadron Officer School, Maxwell AFB, Alabama.

Captain Robert "Kiebs" Kiebler leads this ACC "vic" with Captain Renegar in the Eagle and Captain Shepard in the Viper during the finale photo flight from Nellis AFB using the B-25 as the camera ship.

The most incredible thing I've done in the A-10 Warthog - more than shooting the 30mm gatlin gun - more than flying low through desert canyons - has been leading formations of war birds at air shows around the country. I feel like I've traveled back in time when I glance to my left and right wing and see Mustangs, Lightnings, Sabers and the original Thunderbolt. The big props spinning, - the unmistakable droning of war bird engines - the colorful paint schemes - all next to an A-10, compress the history of the air force into one amazing formation. I'm extremely honored to be a part of the Heritage Flight program and thankful each time we fly these amazing sorties.

Like most Hog drivers, I have a lot experiences that I'm very proud of and look back on with fondness. Unlike many other airplanes, Hog drivers are in a very exclusive club. With no 2-seaters in the inventory, the only people who have been airborne in the Hog, are Hog drivers themselves - no passengers - no photographers - no big time politician or Hollywood elites; just the Hog drivers. We have unique experiences to draw on

for our conversations at the bar. Each of us remembers with excitement the first time we took off in the A-10. When the gear came up – that was it – you were committed. It's a badge of courage that we in the Hog community are very proud of – the first flight is solo.

It's tough to write anything about the Hog and not mention the 30mm gatlin' gun. Again, its something unique to the Hog community and something we all draw pride from. The question always asked is: What's it like to shoot the gun? I always answer with the facts: the plane shakes a bit, gun gas streams over the canopy and the target gets a beating.

-Capt Eric J. Jachimowicz
Air Force A-10 East Coast Demonstration Team pilot.

Capt Jachimowicz earned a regular commission as a distinguished graduate of Miami University's Reserve Officer Training Corps program in 1993. His first assignment was to Sheppard AFB, TX for Euro-NATO Joint Jet Pilot Training. After earning his wings in May 1995, he moved to Davis-Montham AFB to

qualify in the A-10 Thunderbolt II.

Capt. Jachimowicz was next stationed at Spangdahlem AB, Germany, with the 81st Fighter Squadron. While there, he flew multiple combat sorties over the Former Republic of Yugoslavia in support of Operations Decisive Endeavor and Deliberate Guard. He also deployed to Kuwait and flew sorties in support of the "No-Fly Zone" in Southern Iraq as part of Operation Southern Watch. In 1998, Capt Jachimowicz deployed to Camp Bedrock, Bosnia-Herzegovina.
Before his assignment to the Demonstration Team, Capt Jachimowicz served in the 74th Fighter Squadron, Pope Air Force Base, North Carolina as a Flight Commander and Instructor Pilot.

Capt Jachimowicz is a graduate of the Fighter Electronic Combat Officer Course and a distinguished graduate of Squadron Officer's School. He has over 1,500 hours in the A/OA-10 and has logged over 40 hours of combat time. Capt Jachimowicz is from Dayton, Ohio and is married to the former Jody Lancaster from Bowie, Texas.

Doogie leads the P-38 "Joltin' Josie" flown by Steve Hinton around the desert south of Davis-Monthan AFB during the 2002 Heritage Flight Conference. This flight was a proof of concept mission using an EC-130 flown by the 43rd Electronic Squadron based there at D-M.

Left: Doogie flies close trail to Vlado Lenoch in Moonbeam McSwine during the Indianapolis airshow. The picture was made from the backseat of Brad Hood's P-51 Shangrila. The shot above adds General Bill Anders to the formation at Davis-Monthan.

This page has two images made at Langley AFB. Left was during the C-130 mission and the one on the right is of Captain Eric Jachimowicz making a low pass during his solo demo during the show. The shot on the right was made soon after our dawn takeoff from Nellis with the B-25. The shot is of Captain Robert Kiebler who orchestrated the massive photo-ex from an overhead perch in his Hog. Kiebs acted as on-site air controller to safely coordinate the necessary lead changes needed for the seven separate formation configurations.

Above: Captain Eric Jachimowicz manning-up his jet at the Hanscom AFB show just prior to his flight demo. On the right is Doogie flanked by his ground support teammates SSgt Jason Lynch and SSgt Kris Tatro without whom he would likely never get off the ground. Details next show SSgt Kris Tatro polishing the gun and a little customization of the stowable crew ladder.

Pilot: Capt Eric Jachimowicz
Dcc: SSgt Jason Lynch

Above: Captain Eric Jachimowicz flies off the wing of Brad Hood after a photo mission with Vlado Lenoch during the Indianapolis airshow.

The shot on the right was made at NAS Oceana and gives a good look at the steam gauges of the A-10s rudimentary cockpit.

The detail shot on the left gives you an idea of what the last thing an enemy tank driver sees just before the lights go out.

The far page shows Captain Robert Kiebler as seen from the B-25 on the initial climb out from Nellis AFB just after sunrise. His ground crew flanks "Kiebs" on the ramp later that day at Nellis.

F-16 FIGHTING FALCON

With ground attack capabilities rivaling those of purpose-built strike aircraft, the F-16 Fighting Falcon has distinguished itself as a superior multi-role fighter over its nearly thirty year career. On the eve of the introduction of the Joint Strike Fighter, Viper pilots are all hoping to be around long enough to make the transition to the Air Force's next generation front line fighter.

This shot was made during the Fargo Airshow with Captain Scott Shephard from the B-25 Lady Luck. We flew around looking for good light and when the clouds had settled in as overcast, Bulit decided we should try some afterburner climbs to see if we could salvage the mission. His expert airmanship with the Viper is evident with this series of blower passes.

So what's it like to fly the Viper? I'm Captain Scott "Bulit" Shepard and that's the question I'm most frequently asked at an air show. The way I describe it is a cross between a ride on the most phenomenal roller coaster at Disney Land and a Space Shuttle launch!

From a dead stop, and in a distance less than that of four football fields, I'm airborne and accelerating through 175 miles per hour in a plane weighing more than 14 tons. I've taken the F-16 straight up from 300 feet to five miles high above a crowd of thousands and still rolled out with more speed than most racecar drivers ever see. Speaking of racecars, the jet I'm lucky enough to fly has more horsepower than the entire starting lineup at the Indianapolis 500 – what a monster!

Now I haven't been to space, but a couple of gentlemen that I fly with in the Heritage Flight program have; so I feel I can relate somewhat. How cool is that? How many guys can say they went flying with Bill Anders, Apollo 8 astronaut? What an honor! I've flown with Major General (retired) Bill Anders more than

any of the other twelve Heritage Pilots. We've formed our formation over Peugeot Sound and raced into Lake Washington to fly for hundreds of thousands of people in Seattle, Washington. What a rush! But wait, it gets better…One of the best times I had was flying for 3,000 people in Tucumcari, New Mexico (Yes, Tucumcari, NM!). On this show I was fortunate enough to get teamed up with Colonel (retired) Frank Borman for the Heritage Flight. Colonel Borman was mission commander for Apollo 8 and was one of three men to be the first to orbit the moon. Between the unrivaled hospitality of the people at Tucumcari and hearing first hand what it's like to see the earth rise from the dark side of the moon, it's a place I'll never forget.

I've flown nearly the speed of sound at 300 feet over Lake Shore Drive in downtown Chicago for 1.2 million people. In fact, the Cubs game going on that day stopped and everyone rose to their feet to see the Viper fly by. I've flown 10 hours from Miami, Florida to Santiago, Chile to perform at the largest air show in Central and South America. People ask how I can stand to be cramped in

cockpit similar to that of a sports car for so long? I even wondered myself, but when you see the sunset over the Pacific off your right wing and the Andes towering over 20,000 feet above the sea just off your left wing, it makes all the leg cramps vanish.

Where are the best shows is a question on everyone's mind period. From Canada to South America and from California to Washington D.C., they're all great in one-way or another. Of course I'll never forget the scene of my grand father, a WWII veteran, waving a huge American Flag on the beach of Lake Michigan welcoming my wingman and I back to the Traverse City Cherry Festival and the place I spent my summers as a kid. Or the time my flight crossed a desert canyon northeast of Phoenix, Arizona and all the guys on the fishing boat stood up and raised their beverages to us. And while the view of the Grand Canyon from the edge of the South Rim is indeed spectacular, it's absolutely unbeatable to see from above in the world's most maneuverable fighter.

How cool is it to fly the F-16??? Pretty

This shot is of Captain Shepard over the Nellis range with Bill Anders and Frank Borman in their Mustangs. Both aircraft were designed essentially for the same mission, fighter interdiction and light strike capabilities. The Viper has been vastly improved with the multi-role strike capabilities due to the integration of the LANTIRN target acquisition pod.

Made during the same overcast photo mission at Fargo, this picture shows Captain Shepard pulled up along side of the B-25 where I was able to shoot from the emergency hatch on the right side.

damn cool I'd have to say! I'm fortunate. People always ask me if there were anything I'd rather do? While professional athletes make much more money and are far better known than your run-of-the-mill fighter pilot, I'd rather be me. Flying fighters for the greatest country in the world is something money can't buy and while our days are long, we're often far away from home, and it sure wasn't easy to get where I am today; some moments make it all worth while.

- Captain Scott "Bulit" Shepard
12th Air Force F-16 Demonstration Pilot
Captain Scott "Bulit" Shepard commands the 12th Air Force F-16 Demonstration Team operating out of the 4th Fighter Squadron, Hill Air Force Base, Utah.

He has flown 1100 hours in military jet aircraft, has logged 15 combat hours in support of United Nations initiatives over Iraq for Operation SOUTHERN WATCH, and has recently flown multiple Combat Air Patrol sorties over the western United Sates in support of Operation Nobel Eagle.

Captain Shepard was commissioned in 1992 after graduating from the University of Colorado. He spent the first three years of his career as an Accounting and Finance Officer stationed at Lajes Field, Portugal and McClellan Air Force Base, California. Captain Shepard graduated from Specialized Undergraduate Pilot Training in 1996 at Vance Air Force Base, Oklahoma. He then trained in the F-16 at Luke AFB, Arizona and was thereafter assigned to Kunsan Air Base, Korea for one year. Captain Shepard has been stationed at Hill AFB, Utah since 1998.

Captain Shepard's family has a military tradition dating back to the Civil War. A great great grandfather was in the 15th Michigan Infantry. During WWI his great grandfather served in the Coast Guard patrolling the Great Lakes and Atlantic Ocean. His grandfather, an infantry officer, and grandmother, an Army Nurse, served in the European and Pacific Theatres respectively during WWII. His father, Colonel Donald Shepard, retired from the Air Force in April 1997. Captain Shepard is now the fifth generation to serve his country.

Both of these shots were made from the B-25 Lady Luck during the Fargo air show and depict Captain Scott "Bulit" Shepard maneuvering the F-16 for the camera. The relatively slow speed of the B-25 allows Bulit to enter the "dirty" configuration of gear and flaps down without any deviation from normal airspeed parameters.

This top image is simply a variation of the formation seen earlier with General Anders, Col. Borman and Captain Shepard over the Nevada desert during the Nellis shoot. The shot on the opposite page is Built once again rushing over the farmland outside of Fargo, North Dakota.

This page shows Lee Launderback and Captain Ed "Pinto" Casey chasing Larry Kelly's B-25 Panchito out over the water near NAS Oceana where the two were performing the Heritage Flight formations for the air show. The B-25 was flown this day by Paul Nuwer and Jerry Jeffers.

Captain Edward Daniel Casey, Callsign: "PINTO"

Capt. Edward Daniel Casey is the Air Combat Command F-16 East Coast Demonstration Team Pilot and Commander. As the demonstration pilot, he is responsible for showcasing America's premier multi-role fighter, the F-16 Fighting Falcon, to more than seven million people at more than 65 shows around the world. The captain is currently assigned as a combat mission-ready F-16 pilot with the 20th Fighter Wing, Shaw Air Force Base, S.C.

Capt. Casey was born July 4, 1973 in Brooklyn, N.Y. He graduated from Sparta High School in Sparta, N.J. in 1991. In 1995, the captain entered the Air Force upon graduating from the United States Air Force Academy, Colorado Springs, Colorado.

Top left shows the F-16 East demo team from left to right: SSgt Craig Foust, MSgt Greg Bobzin, Capt. Ed Casey, Capt. Rob Campbell, SSgt Craig Zinck, SSgt Brian McRory. Above you can see Lee Lauderback in his TF-51 Crazy Horse leading Capt. Casey behind Panchito, the B-25 camera ship owned by Larry Kelly and flown by Paul Nuwer and Jerry Jeffers. The picture was made just off the beach at the Oceana air show in Virginia Beach. Left is a shot of SSgt Craig Zinck marshalling Pinto back into the hot ramp after the demo at Oceana.

The shots above are all variations in the formations made during the Nellis photo missions where Captain Shephard had the lead. It is a nice study of the different eras of Air Force fighter and ground attack designs that have helped insure our freedoms and victories. The shot on the right is of Captain Scott Shephard himself taken just after we landed at Nellis.

F-15 EAGLE

Designed as the ultimate air superiority weapon platform in the early 1970's, the F-15 Eagle continues to dominate all aspects of aerial intervention when it comes to American foreign diplomacy. The Eagle proved so effective in the interceptor role that significant export orders have placed the Eagle around the globe in the nations of Saudi Arabia, Japan and Israel.

This wonderful formation took place out over Lake Winnebago during the EAA Convention at Oshkosh. Leading is Captain Lendy Renegar with Frank Borman and Brad Hood in trail. The clouds on this flight were amazing and the lighting that resulted was rare indeed.

My name is major Dan Blue and as one of two ACC F-15 Eagle flight demonstration pilots, I have been afforded some unique opportunities and experiences that I would like to share with you.

Flying with Col. Borman:

My crew chief was helping me strap into the F-15 cockpit, and I looked down at the relatively tiny P-51 parked next to me. Col. Borman and his crew chief were following the same ritual, the time when pilots and crew chiefs exchange last-minute words of confidence, wise cracks, and the first trickle of adrenaline. We were going to taxi out together, then I would be his wingman for the Heritage Flight following the F-15 demo.

All strapped in, time to start setting up the 269 switches before engine start. I looked down at Col. Borman and he was also throwing switches. For a moment I imagined we were in the Apollo 8 capsule together, running pre-flight checklists as we prepared to become the first men to leave the Earth for the Moon. Then my mind raced back to that Christmas Eve in 1968, when I was 6 years old, and my family crowded around a radio to hear the voices of the crew of Apollo 8. They circled the moon and read from Genesis, and I can still hear the echoes of Col. Borman's last transmission:

"And from the crew of Apollo 8, we close with good night, good luck, a Merry Christmas, and God bless all of you – all of you on the good Earth."

I remember looking up at the moon that night and the spark within that grew into a passion for flying. Back in the P-51, Col. Borman was cranking the Mustang. I got back to my own checklist, thinking, " I'd better be a damn good wingman today."

Flying the F-15 demo:

My favorite part is staring down the hot runway, pre-flight checks complete, no sound but the low rumble of the two idling Pratt & Whitney F-100 afterburning turbofans I'm strapped to. I get the "run 'em up" call from my guy at show center as the narrator has almost finished the intro. The adrenaline is now coursing through the veins with full force as I run up the engines to 80%. The F-15 creaks and groans, almost complaining that I'm still holding the brakes. I hear "release brakes", and slam the throttles forward to full afterburner. The Eagle happily responds to her new found freedom, forcing me further back in the ejection seat as each of five afterburner stages ignite. I'm now rocketing down the runway, "hair on fire", on the way to what we like to call "15 minutes of fun."

The Photo Missions

Pilots are always asked, "What's it like to _____?" by those less fortunate earthbound souls. I can describe the physiological sensations of flying high-performance aircraft, the gut-wrenching centrifuge of a swirling dogfight. Or the satisfaction of achieving complete symbiosis with a machine as powerful and lethal as the F-15.

Captain Lendy Renegar breaks right after completing our photo mission with the B-25 over Lacrosse, Wisconsin.

Over the shimmering waters of Lake Michigan, Major Dan Blue leads Dale Snodgrass and Reg Urschler in the "vic" formation of Mustangs behind the B-25 Lady Luck. For Major Blue, flying at Muskegon is like coming home and he had a great turnout of friends and family who came to watch him perform.

I can tell people about the sights I've seen from the cockpit of the Eagle: the unbelievable hell of a hundred burning Kuwaiti oil wells; looking straight down into an erupting volcano surrounded by the frozen vastness of Iceland; a surface-to-air missile launching toward you on a pitch-black desert night. I can describe the awe of leading an eight-ship formation of highly trained Eagle Drivers, dealing in death, breaking MACH below a dark overcast while ten-foot ocean swells rage below.

The emotion of flying armed escort for Air Force One as it flew the president to ground zero, and patrolling overhead while trying to ignore the smoking devastation below. The honor and privilege of flying in formation with some of the greatest pilots and airplanes that have served this country so well.

Some things however, are simply beyond description. Besides the sights burned into my memory during a mission, the true art of our formation flying can only be brought back

to others on film, and that's what this book is about.

Erik Hildebrandt has captured some aerial scenes that a rare few will ever see in person — four generations of America's definitive warplanes flying together in a tribute to Air Force heritage. These airplanes are more than just a beautiful sight; they represent America's commitment to quality in aviation that is unmatched by any nation in the world. They also represent the thousands who gave their lives in the air defending freedom, and those who continue to serve.

The Heritage Flight is a visual reminder that our freedom has come at a cost, paid by men and machines, and that aviation will always play a vital role in protecting our nation.

Major Daniel S. Blue is the United States Air Force East Coast F-15 aerial demonstration pilot based at the 1st Fighter Wing, Langley Air Force Base, Va.
As aerial demonstration pilot, he is responsible for representing Air Com-

bat Command, the United States Air Force and the Department of Defense. He commands the 12-member East Coast demonstration team and performs F-15 demonstrations at some 30 show locations for more than 10 million spectators annually. He plans, organizes and schedules team deployment to worldwide air show locations and manages the team's $100,000 annual budget.
Major Blue was commissioned through Officer Training School at Lackland Air Force Base, Texas, following graduation from the University of Michigan in 1987. Upon graduation he attended the flight screening program at Hondo, Texas.
His career includes duties as an F-15 pilot and instructor, as well as a T-38 instructor at Euro-North Atlantic Treaty Organization Joint Jet Pilot Training.
Prior to his current assignment, Major Blue was an F-15 instructor pilot in the 27th Fighter Squadron, Langley Air Force Base, Va.
He is a senior pilot with more than 2,300 flying hours, including more than 1,600 in the F-15.

Major Dan Blue pulls up behind the C-130 with Ed Shipley on his wing. Shot during the Langley AFB photo mission, you can see the eastern shore of Maryland in the background. On the opposite page, Major Blue executes a series of high performace afterburner climbs for the camera during the show at Quonset Point.

On this page you can see Major Dan Blue leading Dale Snodgrass and General Reg Urschler out over Lake Michigan during the Muskegon airshow. Snort is flying Excaliber, a Mustang owned by Jim Read while Reg can always be found at the controls of Gunfighter, the famous P-51 owned by the CAF. On the opposite page, Captain Lendy Renegar demonstrates the slow speed handling characteristics of the F-15 in the dirty configuration with gear and flaps down over Lacrosse, Wisconsin. Both shots were made from the B-25.

Demonstrating the breathtaking power of the F-15 Eagles, two Pratt and Whitney F-100 engines in full afterburner, Major Dan Blue goes vertical behind the C-130 out over Long Island Sound during the Quonset Point airshow in Rhode Island.

Clockwise from top left: Major Dan Blue puts his arms around crew chief Sherry "Calli" Callahan after another eye-watering demo at Langley AFB. Major Blue with his crew at Quonset Point : Master Sergeant Sherry Callahan, Tech Sergeant Tyrone "T-Bone" Tillery and Senior Airman Brandon Taylor. Major Blue stretches his body out after a brutal high-G flight demo. Bottom left: Major Blue generates serious contrails at the backside of a burner loop.

Captain Lendy Renegar is the Air Combat Command's F-15 West Coast demonstration Team Pilot and Officer in charge of the F-15 Demonstration Team. As the Demonstration pilot, he is responsible for showcasing America's F-15C to over seven million people at over 65 shows around the world. He is currently assigned as a combat mission ready F-15 pilot with the 33rd Fighter Wing, Eglin AFB, Florida.

Captain Renegar was born May 20, 1972 in Yadkinville, North Carolina. He graduated from Cary, High School in Cary, North Carolina in 1990. In 1994 he earned a Bachelor of Science degree in Meteorology from North Carolina State University, Raleigh, North Carolina. Captain Renegar is currently working on his Masters Degree at Embry Riddle Aeronautical University, Florida

Flight hours: Approx. 800 hours
F-15 Flight Hours: 600
Combat hours: 70 hours
Aircraft flown: T-37, T-38, AT-38, F-15
MAJOR AWARDS AND DECORATIONS:
Air Medal
Aerial Achievement Medal
Air Force Commendation Medal
National Defense Service Medal
Armed Forces Expeditionary Medal

Above: Capt. Renegar presents the Eagle in a high alpha attitude behind the B-25 over Lacrosse, WI. Top Right: Alamo leads Frank Borman and Brad Hood over Lake Winnebago during the EAA Convention at Oshkosh. Below left to right: Capt. Renegar and MSgt. Marquis Salley, safety officer Capt. Paul O'Brien, and ground crew Kenny Lloyd, Lonnie Gore, and Jeremy Wilson

THUNDERBIRDS

It seems amazing that of the hundred years since man first took to the skies, fifty of those have seen performances by the Air Force's Thunderbirds. Officially acitivated on June 1, 1953 at Luke AFB as the 3600th Air Demonstration Flight, the name Thunderbirds was chosen to reflect the native American influences of the region.

Photographed in the Delta formation on the range over Death Valley, California, the Thunderbirds joined up on the C-130J from the 143rd AW at Quonset Point, Rhode Island before the Nellis AFB airshow.

The current U.S. Air Force flight demonstration team, the "Thunderbirds," had its beginning in 1953, when Brigadier General Charles Born, commander of crew training, was given the task of forming a unit "to demonstrate efficiency, familiarization and orientation to people not knowing of the F-84G; to create interest in the training program; and to recruit aviation cadets".

The 3600th Air Demonstration Flight was officially established at Luke AFB, Arizona on June 1, 1953. The team needed an aircraft that was stable for formation flight, reliable enough to meet the demanding show schedule, rugged enough for aerobatic maneuvers, and representative of the Air Force's combat aircraft, and the Republic F-84G Thunderjet was chosen.

Next came the task of selecting the first team pilots, which eventually included team leader Major Dick Catledge, wingmen Lts. Bill and Buck Pattillo (formerly of the "Skyblazers"), and slotman Captain Bob Kanaga. The next task was to select a name for the team, and a contest was held at Luke AFB.
The name "Stardusters" was selected from the entries received, but this selection was overruled by the commander of the Air Training Command, who insisted that the name "Thunderbirds" was more appropriate because of the Native American heritage of the area around Luke AFB. To the Native Americans, the Thunderbird grants victory in war by controlling the forces of good over evil. Captain Bob McCormick, the team's spare pilot, designed the red, white, and blue color scheme to be applied to the F-84G Thunderjets and the team's emblem, both of which have changed little since 1953.

The "Thunderbirds" flew their first demonstration on June 8, 1953 to an audience of 3,000 at Luke AFB and its first public airshow eight days later. In 1954, the "Thunderbirds" made a 12-country tour of Central and South America, featuring a supersonic show opening by a solo performer in an F-86 Sabre.

In keeping with the mission of showcasing the Air Force's top-of-the-line fighter aircraft, in 1955 the "Thunderbirds" switched to the Republic F-84F Thunderstreak, a swept-wing version of the Thunderjet. Smoke tanks were added to the Thunderstreaks, and the new air show regularly featured a solo performer in addition to the traditional diamond formation maneuvers.

For the 1956 airshow season, the "Tbirds" again changed aircraft, this time to the North American F-100C Super Sabre. The Super Sabre gave the "Thunderbirds" the distinction of being the first flight demonstration team with supersonic capability. The change allowed the team to greatly expand its airshow, with more climbing maneuvers than were possible before.

In 1956, the team was transferred to Nellis AFB, Nevada, which has been its home base ever since. The team suffered one of the most devastating crashes in its history in October 1958, when a C-123 support aircraft crashed, killing 14 support members. The "Thunderbirds" made their first Far East tour in 1959, performing 29 shows in 31 days and also demonstrating the long-range deployment capabilities of the Air Force. President John F. Kennedy was among the spectators at a May 1962 airshow at Eglin AFB, Florida, and in 1963, the "Tbirds" made their first European and North African tours.

In 1964, the "Thunderbirds" transitioned to the Republic F-105 Thunderchief. However, this change lasted only six shows during the period of April 26 to May 9. On May

Made during the same photo flight as the opening shot and now transitioned to the 4-ship Diamond, Thunderbirds 1 through 4 executed a variety of formations that are typical of their normal flight demonstrations as seen from the ground. While a few pictures like this have been snapped during their frequent aerial refueling events crossing the country to airshows, the team had never before flown behind a C-130 for the purpose of a dedicated photo mission. Many thanks to the pilots but to Lt. Col. McSpadden especially for trusting that not only could we execute a safe flight, but that it would be worth everyone's effort.

Thunderbirds

Thunderbirds 5 and 6 are considered the lead and opposing solos. Here #5, Major Shawn "Norm" Pederson forms up on #7 Glenn "Lunar" Lawson flying us around in the F-16 camera ship as #6, Captain Todd "Tales" Canterbury breaks high and right in a series of orchestrated maneuvers for the camera. Normally you only see these two guys heading straight towards each other at breath-taking closure rates.

9th, Captain Gene Devlin's Thunderchief broke apart during a climb due to structural problems, and all Air Force Thuderchiefs were immediately grounded until the problem could be fixed. However, the "Thunderbirds" never used the Thundercheif again, instead switching to the F-100D, an upgraded version of the F-100C Super Sabres they had used from 1956 to 1963. For the "Thunderbirds," the F-100D era (1964 to 1968) was, and continues to hold the record as, the busiest in the team's history.

In 1967, the "Thunderbirds" flew their 1000th show, and in 1968 the team was officially designated the U.S. Air Force Air Demonstration Squadron.

In 1969 the "Thunderbirds" were given the McDonnell-Douglas F-4E Phantom II, the top-of-the-line fighter aircraft at the time, as its new show plane. The 1969 the team flew over the graduating class of the Air Force Academy which was broadcast by ABC television to more than 10 million viewers nationwide.

In contrast, the team performed to its smallest audience, 30 people, at Clear, Alaska in 1969 and in 1971 performed to its largest audience ever, more than 2.3 million in two days at the Paris Airshow at Le Bourget Airport.

As the oil crisis of 1973 strangled America's economy, "efficiency" became the key-word in the selection by the "Thunderbirds" of the Northrop T-38 Talon as the replacement for the F-4E Phantom. The Talon is the only non-combat aircraft used by the team, but it was unequalled in terms of economy: five Talons used the same amount of fuel for an airshow as one Phantom!

On January 18, 1982, a malfunction on the leaders' aircraft during a line abreast loop caused the entire team to crash into the Nevada desert during a practice airshow. Despite public cries to discontinue military flight demo teams, Congress passed a resolution on January 26, 1982, stating that "The Congress hereby affirms its strong support for continuation of the Thunderbirds program."

1982 was a year of rebuilding for the "Thunderbirds." The team took deliver of its first General Dynamics F-16 Fighting Falcon and spent the next 10 months practicing in preparation for the 1983 show season. About 16 million spectators in 33 states saw the "Tbirds" in action, including a record 2.4 million for a 1-day show at Coney Island. The team made its first appearance in a Communist country in 1987, with a Far East tour that included shows in the People's Republic of China. The team upgraded to the F-16C variant of the Fighting Falcon (from the original F-16A variant) in 1992, and celebrated its 40th Anniversary in 1993. In 1996, the "Thunderbirds" made another European tour, this one including shows in the former Soviet-bloc countries of Romania, Bulgaria, and Slovenia.

By December 1999, the "Thunderbirds" had been in existence for 46 years and had performed shows in 59 countries and all 50 states for more than 290 million people worldwide.

As the world celebrates the Centennial of Flight in 2003, the fact that the team has been a part of the history of aviation for fully one half of those 100 years is lost on no one at the Thunderbirds. Today as they did yesterday and are sure to do tomorrow, the men and women of the U.S. Air Force Thunderbirds will carry on the traditions of excellence as they are all truly America's Ambassadors to the world.

-Arnold E. van Beverhoudt, Jr

Left: The solos reposition themselves over the practice range at Indian Springs where the Thunderbirds do most of their home field rehearsing. Above is a unique overhead view of the underside of the Thunderbird Diamond formation as Boss takes the guys over the top of the Diamond loop. The lines visible below are simply roads carved out of the desert floor that the team uses the same way as they do show line references while on the road.

The top of this page depicts the very instant that the solos "hit" during their knife edge pass. I made this shot in the backseat of #7 with Lunar flying a loose shadow position on Norm. Left to right on this page shows #5 Shawn Pederson cranking the Viper across the open ramp of the C-130J over Death Valley. The next two shots were made at Eau Claire, Wisconsin and show Norm in full blower as he pulls off high and right to rejoin the diamond and the solos during their mirror pass. Right page: The Delta trails smoke behind the C-130J over Death Valley.

This page shows an image I made while the team was setting up for an initial air start just outside of the practice range over Indian Springs. This range is only about twenty miles from Nellis and affords the team much less congested airspace as well as a sparsely populated practice area. The opposite page is yet another formation variation from the C-130J photo mission. This time, Boss has positioned the team in a tight trailing stack that clearly demonstrates the incredible precision for which the Thunderbirds are renowned. Top right on that page was made at Quonset Point. The lower right shot was made during the Diamond Loop as the team is driving up hill towards the apex.

The shot on this page mirrors with the top image on the opposite page. Both show the 4-ship echelon pass in review as seen from a close chase in #7 as well as the view from the crowd line. The shots across the bottom of the opposite page are some of the various formations flown by the Thunderbirds: the two on the left are both ground to air shots of the Delta, while the remaining three were made during the chase flight and the C-130J photo mission around Nellis AFB.

P-38 LIGHTNING

The brainchild of legendary Lockheed designer Kelly Johnson, the P-38 Lightning saw action in every theater of operation during the Second World War. Plagued by developmental hurdles precipitated by its complexity and unprecedented performance, the Lightning went on to generate the two highest scoring American aces of the War: Richard Bong and Thomas McGuire.

As the first twin tailed American fighter, the P-38 was designed for the same basic mission as the twin tailed F-15 Eagle. This shot was taken from the tail gunner psoition of the B-25 Lady Luck over the mountains just north of Las Vegas, Nevada. The Lightning is being flown by Steve Hinton while Lendy Renegar is flying the Eagle

There were a total of 10,038 Lightnings produced in support of World War II at an average cost of about $100,000 each. A total of 9925 were produced by Lockheed Burbank, the LOs, and 113 were produced by Consolidated Vultee in Nashville and were identified as VNs.

There were a total of 708 G models manufactured and 548 were modified in Dallas for arctic conditions and identified as –10s. When first manufactured as a high altitude interceptor in 1941, the P-38 was far superior to any United States manufactured fighter.

It had a service ceiling of over 16 thousand feet, would exceed 400 MPH and had a range of up to 1500 miles with 20 minutes of combat time. Its contemporaries only had a service ceiling of 12 thousand feet and could only reach about 230 MPH with a range of less than 500 miles.

The P-38 essentially carried the land based war in the Pacific Theater as it was the only aircraft with the range to carry out the island hopping strategy used to defeat Japan. The top two all time aces of the Army Air Corps, Major Richard Bong with 40 kills and Major Thomas McGuire with 38 kills both flew P-38s.

Another advantage that the P-38 had over its contemporaries was that four 50 caliber machine guns and one 20 millimeter canon were all mounted in the nose giving a concentrated firepower. Single engine fighters had the guns mounted in the wings, which produced crossing fire.

The first P-38 kills of the war were on August 4, 1942 when Lt Stanley Long and Lt Kenneth Ambrose of the 54th Fighter Squadron shot down two Japanese Mavis flying boats near Atka in the Aleutian Islands of Alaska.
The P-38 Lightning resulted from an Army Air Corps specification issued in 1936 for a high altitude twin engine interceptor with a maximum speed of 360 miles per hour at 20,000 feet. The first flight of the radically different fighter took place on January 1939. It was the first military plane to be developed by Lockheed and the first of many to be designed by the famous "Skunk Works" team headed by Kelly Johnson.

Powered by two turbo super-charged Allison in-line engines, the twin boomed fighter boasted an awesome armament of four 50 caliber machine guns and one 20 millimeter cannon mounted in the nose to give the fighter parallel line of fire.

The Lightning served in every World War II Theater of operations and was used extensively as a long-range escort fighter. A very versatile aircraft, it also used for level and dive bombing and ground strafing. The Lightning was produced in 14 models beginning with the XP-38 and ending with the P-38M, a P-38L modified as a night

With General Bill Anders pulling off the runway behind him, Steve Hinton taxis the P-38 Lightning back to the ramp after the dual Heritage Flight Formations at Nellis AFB. The sounds of the twin Alison engines are unlike any other plane and is yet one more distinction that sets the Lightning apart as a true one of kind design.

In a formation unlike many flown before, Steve Hinton leads this wonderful finger-four ship including Bill Anders in the Mustang, Lendy Renegar in the Eagle and Dale Snodgrass in the F-86. This photo was taken from the B-25 during a 10-ship master flight out of Nellis that included an A-10, 2 Mustangs, a P-47, a F-86, a F-16, a F-15 a P-38, the B-25 and a C-130J. The shot on the opposite page is a variation of this same formation.

fighter. A photo reconnaissance version, the F-5, was also built.

The P-38G located at Elmendorf Air Force Base was delivered April 3, 1943, by air from the Lockheed factory at Burbank, California, to Lockheed's Dallas Modification Center for winterization.

It was then flown to Elmendorf Field on May 18, arriving there on May 28, where it was assigned to the 54th Fighter Squadron, 343rd Fighter Group, Eleventh Air Force. It may have participated in the Aleutian Campaign, which ended August 15, 1943, with the reoccupation of Kiska Island.

The 54th Fighter Squadron was the first squadron to operationally employ the P-38, and the only P-38 unit in Alaska. The squadron arrived in Alaska shortly after the Japanese bombed U.S. naval base at Dutch Harbor and occupied Attu and Kiska Islands in the Aleutians Islands in early June 1942. The squadron was

equipped with the early model P-38E at the time.

Because of the Lightning's 1,100 mile range and twin engine capability, the squadron drew most of the difficult fighter mission during the campaign. The 54th Fighter Squadron claimed the first P-38 aerial victory of the war when two of its pilots shot down two Japanese flying boats over Atka Island on August 4, 1942.

Of the original complement of 30 pilots that deployed to the Aleutians in June 1942, 17 lost their lives by the time the Aleutian Campaign ended August 15, 1943

The 54th was the only squadron equipped with the P-38 during the Aleutian Campaign, and was based on Amchitka in the Aleutians at the time. Later the squadron moved to Alexei Field, Attu Island where it provided air defense of western bases in the Aleutians.

On the right is another shot of the trail stack lead by Steve Hinton in the P-38. Top this page is Steve manning up for the sunrise launch out of Nellis. Above is the finsihed product of the Heritage Flight as seen by the air show crowd.

The Heritage Flight formation as seen during the Nellis show captures the majesty of what the program is all about: American ingenuity and determination to produce the means to defend freedom and afford her soldiers and pilots the best possible machines with which to accomplish that mission.

The top image is yet another background variation from the same formation series; they each hold their own special appeal. The series along the bottom from left to right is Steve Hinton getting ready to fly at Nellis. The cockpit of the P-38 illustrates the bomber style yolk instead of a stick as is found in most fighters. The shot on the bottom right is of General Howie Chandler getting stuffed into the minimal "backseat" of the P-38 for a truly once in a lifetime experience with Steve Hinton. The two shots on the right page are photo studies of the graceful lines of the Lightning.

P-47 THUNDERBOLT

Nicknamed the "jug" for its milk bottle appearance, the P-47 Thunderbolt was far and away the most rugged fighter of World War Two. Stories abound of its ability to absorb battle damage which ironically enough, was sometimes inflicted by her own doing. Pilots drove the plane so low on strafing runs that the debris from exploding munitions would be blown directly into the flight path. Besides tree branches and leaves, a pilot once reported removing part of telephone pole from his engine cowling.

A rare shot of the two Thunderbolts both produced by Republic Aircraft on Long Island. While their shapes are vastly different, their respective missions and reputations remain the same: heavy hitting ground pounders that strike fear into the hearts of those unfortunate enough to see them from this angle. Shot over Nevada desert.

The Republic P-47 Thunderbolt was a fighter designed in 1939-1940 by two Russian engineers, naturalized North American, Alexander de Seversky and Alexander Kartveli. A former bomber pilot in the Imperial Russian Navy, Seversky had lost a leg in combat but nonetheless continued flying, using an artificial limb. While on a visit to the U.S.A. with the Soviet Naval Mission in 1918, he defected and was granted political asylum.

He soon became an aeronautical advisor to the U.S. War Department. In 1931, he founded the Seversky Aircraft Corporation, in Farmingdale, Long Island, New York. Hiring Kartveli as engineer, they both designed some aircraft, among which the SEV-1XP, which outperformed the Curtiss P-36 Hawk in a competition promoted in 1936 by the U.S. Army Air Corps - U.S.A.A.C..

Known by the military designation P-35, it was the first modern U.S. Army fighter, incorporating a metal fuselage, low set wings, a retractable landing gear (though the wheels did not flush completely into the wings) and a radial Pratt&Whitney R-1830 engine delivering 850HP.

In 1939, Seversky designed the XP-41, incorporating a cleaner-designed fuselage (whose back portion was higher than in the P-35, going straight from the end of the cockpit to join the fin, a profile that became known as razorback); a completely retractable landing gear; two .30in machine guns on the engine cowling; and a P&W R-1830 coupled to a compressor delivering 1,150HP which allowed it to reach a speed of 320MPH at 15,000ft. However, its performance did not impress the U.S.A.A.C. officials and it was suggested to Seversky to use a turbocompressor, which had already been in use by the Boeing B-17 bombers.

Seversky and Kartveli then modified the fuselage of XP-41, to accommodate the turbocompressor in its rear portion, with the necessary piping passing underneath the cockpit; weaponry was also increased to house two .50in machine guns in the wings. The new aircraft received the designation YP-43 Lancer and was able to reach 350MPH and an altitude of 38,000ft, the first YP-43 was being delivered in September 1940.

At the same time, Seversky and Kartveli proposed the XP-44, which presented a more aerodynamic cabin, and a propeller cube to reduce the aerodynamic drag caused by the large frontal area of the high power radial engine chosen. Having planned to use the 1,400HP P&W R-2180, they were forced to choose the 2,000 HP P&W XR-2800 "Double Wasp" when the first was cancelled. The projected performance for the XP-44 were so impressive that the U.S.A.A.C. ordered 80 aircraft even before a prototype had been built. However, with the fall of France the order was cancelled, as the XP-44 was considered to be inferior to the German Messerschmitt Bf-109.

In the meantime, so as to avoid the closure of the Seversky Aircraft Company, the U.S.A.A.C. ordered 54 P-43As, to which another 80 were added when the XP-44 was cancelled. In July 1941, Nationalist China acquired 125 P-43s, of which 108 were delivered - the remaining 13 being impressed into U.S.A.A.C. use after 7 December 1941. These were converted to perform photo reconnaissance missions under the designation of P-43B. Also, four P-43As and four P-43Ds were used by two units of the Royal Australian Air Force in the photo reconnaissance rôle over the South Pacific.

With the cancellation of the XP-44, Seversky and Kartveli proposed a new fighter, known by the company as the "Advanced Pursuit design

Tommy Gregory pulls out of the chocks at Nellis to go fly the Heritage Flight for the airshow. This P-47 was previously owned by Charles Osborn of Vintage Fighters and was painted up as Big Ass Bird. Today the plane is owned and operated by the Lone Star Flight Museum in Galveston, Texas.

A late afternoon photo mission with Tom Gregory during the EAA Convention in Oshkosh resulted in this solo shot of the P-47 over the Wisconsin countryside. It does not take too much imagination to see the farms below as those of the western European theater where the Jug saw most of her action during WWII.

no. 10" (AP-10), and as the XP-47 by the U.S.A.A.C.. This new design should have been powered by the in line, liquid-cooled Allison V-1710; however, the U.S.A.A.C. soon asked for the introduction of items to satisfy its requirements: a heavier armament, self-sealing fuel tanks, armor protection for the pilot and under wing pylons, among others. This led to an increase in the aircraft weight and by May 1940 it all looked as if it would be cancelled.

Thus in September 1940 Seversky and Karveli proposed a different design for the XP-47, based on their experience with the SEV-1XP. The new fighter would be powered by the double-row, 18 cylinder, turbocompressor charged 2,000HP P&W R-2800; it would have an armored cockpit and a heavy armament comprising eight .50in machine guns, four in each wing. Its speed would exceed 400MPH and would reach a ceiling close to 40,000ft.

In fact, the XP-47 was designed around the engine and turbocompressor system. The turbocompressor itself was mounted behind the pilot, the necessary piping passing beneath the cockpit from the engine to the turbocompressor and back. The enormous dimensions of the new fighter - "it will be a dinosaur, but a dinosaur with good proportions", according to Kartveli - were dictated by that very power system. The first flight was accomplished on 6 May 1941 and, after fixing some problems, the mass production of the P-47 began, and eventually 15,682 would be built by war's end. The prototype XP-47 had a fixed canopy, with the cockpit access through a car-type door.

The first versions - P-47B, C, D-1 to D-23 and G (variant C built by Curtiss) - had the "razorback" fuselage and a rear-sliding, heavily framed canopy, which made it difficult to look rearwards. Starting from the D-25 version, a bubble hood offering unrestricted vision was installed on a cut out rear fuselage, these versions becoming known as "bubble top" (the first P-47 modified as such was known as the XP-47K). The loss of directional stability caused by the cut out rear fuselage led to the fitting of a dorsal fin fillet ahead of the empennage; this modification was introduced in the production line from the D-40 version onwards and retrofitted to the other "bubble top" variants when major servicing was due.

The P-47M version was developed to obtain a better performance, to enable the Thunderbolt to regain its superiority over the latest German fighters introduced from 1944 onwards. It was equipped with a more powerful engine and had its armament reduced to six .50in machine guns. A single U.S. Army Air Forces fighter group was equipped with this variant.

The last version that saw operational service was the N, which was developed to be used in the Pacific Theatre of Operations. It was optimized to have a greater endurance, in order to fly across the vast sea expanses escorting the Boeing B-29 Superfortress bombers on their way to Japan an back. That version was distinguishable from the others for its semi-elliptical wing plan form similar to that of two British-designed fighters, the Hawker Tempest and the Vickers-Supermarine Spitfire Mk. 21) and for a larger dorsal fin fillet.

The Thunderbolt, also known as "Jug" (as it looked like a milk jug) by the British and U.S. personnel and as the "Trator Voador" (flying tractor) by the Brazilians, was used in World War II by the United States, Great-Britain (mainly in Southeast Asia), Free France, Soviet Union, Mexico and Brazil. After the war, it was also used by the air forces of Bolivia, Chile, Nationalist China, Colombia, Ecuador, Honduras, Iran, Italy, Yugoslavia, Nicaragua, Peru, Portugal, Dominican Republic, Turkey and Venezuela.

-Rudnei Dias da Cunha

The opposite page shows Tom Gregory breaking off from the B-25 to RTB the warbird ramp at Oshkosh over Lake Winnebago. This page is the pre-dawn preparation for the mass gaggle photo mission at Nellis AFB. In the distance is Lady Luck, the Minneapolis based B-25 responsible for the majority of the missions executed for this project. Nothing beats flying cross country with your good friends on the way to make circles in the sky with the legends that make up the Heritage Flight. Life is good.

In this shot we see Tom Gregory joined by fellow Heritage pilot Reg Urschler over Lake Winnebago along with Tom Wood in his Bearcat and Frank Strickler in Tom's Mustang. The opposite page stares down the noses of the P-47 and the A-10 flown by Tom Gregory and Captain Robert Kiebler during the Nellis photo flight in Lady Luck.

This page shows Tarheel Hal on the warbird ramp at Oshkosh. Opposite page clockwise from top are Tom Gregory and Major John York over Lake Winnebago. The cockpit of the jug as seen on the ramp at Nellis. Tom Gregory smiling after yet another hard day at the office. The results of the Nellis photo mission with a nice shot of Tom sandwiched between as he gets ready to man up just before dawn at Nellis AFB.

P-51 MUSTANG

Designed and built in only four months, the P-51 Mustang was initially intended to be a replacement for the British Hawker Hurricane. As the first fighter ever designed by North American, the Mustang would set in motion a long line of renowned fighters for the company which ultimately would become part of Boeing family of aviation companies.

Photographed over the Atlantic ocean just off the shore of Virginia Beach during the Oceana air show, Lee Lauderback in Crazy Horse leads Captain Edward Casey in the F-16 behind the B-25 Panchito flown by Paul Nuwer and Kevin Smith and owned by Larry Kelly.

In the early months of 1940, America's entry into World War II was still nearly two years away. But on the European continent, nothing seemed to be able to slow the onslaught of the German military as one country after another came under Nazi control. It appeared to be only a matter of time, and perhaps a very short time, before England would be facing the German war machine alone.

Great Britain needed the weapons and materials of war in great quantity, and it needed them quickly. Nothing was of higher priority than fighter planes to defend the island nation, and in January 1940, before the fall of France, the Anglo French Purchasing Commission came to America hoping to acquire additional P-40s. But the Curtiss production lines were operating at capacity, so some "back room" discussions sent them to see James H. "Dutch" Kindelberger, the president of North American Aviation.

The British had purchased aircraft from North American before, but they had been trainers, not the fighters they now so desperately needed. In fact, up to that time, North American had never

produced a true fighter design. During World War II, it would later become common for one company to produce another's design. Vega and Douglas would build Boeing's B-17, Goodyear would build Vought's Corsair, General Motors would build Grumman's Wildcat and Avenger, and Curtiss would even build Republic's Thunderbolts. But in 1940, North American was not interested in producing Curtiss P-40s for the British.

Instead, North American informed the British that it could produce an even better fighter plane than the P40 while still using the same Allison V-171 0 inline engine. Reports have been published stating that North American stipulated in the contract that this would be accomplished in only 120 days, but in fact, there was no such guarantee in the contract. Nevertheless, North American did assure the British that the plane could be designed and produced very quickly.

The NA-73X prototype was ready to fly only sixmonths after design work began. Most of the

major features seen on this aircraft were retained throughout the entire Mustang production run, and this is clear evidence of the excellent planning and sound judgement that went into the design.

On April 10, 1940, the proposal was accepted, and the prototype, assigned North American's model number NA-73, was ordered. The following month, France fell to the Germans, and England was indeed alone. Soon, a small number of Spitfires and Hurricanes would begin the defense of England against the Luftwaffe in the Battle of Britain. Britain's need for fighters was never more desperate.

Asked to name the American military personnel who made significant contributions to victory in World War II, men like Dwight Eisenhower, George Patton, Douglas MacArthur and Chester Nimitz would be on most lists. But a very good argument could also be made to include First Lieutenant Benjamin S. Kelsey. Lt. Kelsey was head of the Army Air Corps Pursuit Projects Office at Wright Field, and he was the single most important man in the acquisition

Jimmy Beasley Jr. flies his dad Jim Beasley Senior's beautifully polished P-51 Mustang "Bald Eagle" over the eastern shore of Maryland on a photo mission launched from Langley AFB. In trail you can see Ed Shipley in his F-86, Major Dan Blue in the F-15 Eagle and Captain Eric Jachimowicz in the A-10 Warthog. In the backseat of Jimmy's plane is General Bruce Wright enjoying the view of the business end of the C-130H camera ship flown by the guys from the 143rd AW at Quonset Point, Rhode Island.

A great view of Brad Hood in the foreground and Frank Borman formed up on the B-25 Lady Luck during our mission at Oshkosh. You can clearly see in this photo the difference in the two tails of these Mustangs. The taller vertical stabilizer on Col. Borman's TF-51 distinguishes it as a later model Mustang that was built as a dual controlled trainer version. A few Mustangs have had dual controls added to original single stick aircraft, but true TF variants were purposely built with two sticks and are vastly superior for actual training. Lee Lauderback's Crazy Horse is also a genuine TF-51 which he still uses for Mustang instruction and checkout flights in his Stallion 51 training operation in Florida.

of what would eventually become the P51 Mustang fighter. With a degree in aeronautical engineering from M.I.T., Kelsey was qualified in aircraft design and performance, and he ingeniously found the means and the money to keep the program going until America's entry into the war ensured its success.

On May 4, 1940, when North American obtained release to sell the NA-73 to the British, Kelsey had included the stipulation that two aircraft from the first production batch would be turned over to Wright Field for testing. This meant that the British would buy the U.S. Army two aircraft which it did not then have the funds to purchase for itself.

Kelsey also knew of the National Advisory Committee on Aeronautics' (the forerunner to NASA) studies on the laminar flow airfoil, and as an aeronautical engineer, he understood its importance to new aircraft design and performance. As a result, NACA's Eastman Jacobs was assigned to North American's team that was working on the new fighter for the British. Raymond H. Rice was North American's chief engineer, Edgar

Schmued their chief of design, and Ed Horkey was the aerodynamicist. Along with Jacobs, they worked day and night, seven days a week, to produce the new fighter as quickly as possible.

Curtiss had been ordered to turn over its design studies and other pertinent information on the XP-46. This included the radiator scoop originally intended for installation under the fuselage of the P-40. This scoop, which provided cooling air for glycol and oil cooling, was also to have a hot air exit ramp which would create thrust that more than offset the drag caused by the frontal cross-section for the scoop.

Though never fitted operationally to the P-40, it held promise and was one of the features incorporated in the design of the NA-73. Just how much the data from Curtiss was used is subject to debate. Curtiss engineers state that it was almost total, while those at North American claim that little of the information was used. The truth is probably somewhere between these two extremes. Clearly, the NA-73 had a lot in common with the XP-46, and a rational analysis would

indicate that the NA-73 could not have been engineered in such a short period of time without considerable use of the Curtiss data. But equally as clear is the original thinking added by the North American design team. Among the most important changes was the addition of the laminar flow wing.

On September 9, 1940, only 102 days after the contract had been signed, the NA-73X prototype was rolled out though still waiting for its engine. The new fighter was named Mustang by the British, and the first British version was designated Mustang I. As soon as it was available, the 1,120hp Allison V-171 0-39 powerplant was installed, and engine and taxi tests began.

On 26 October, Vance Breese lifted the aircraft off the runway for a maiden flight. Testing continued until Paul Balfour was forced to make a deadstick landing. The NA73X flipped over on its back, and it took six weeks to make repairs and get the aircraft ready to fly again. The first production Mustang I soon joined the repaired prototype in the test program, and shortly other Mustangs were heading for England.

-Bertram Kinzey; DETAIL & SCALE, Inc.

The opposite page shows Brad Hood in the lead with Col. Borman in SuSu II and Lendy Renegar in the F-15 sliding left into a "vic" formation behind Lady Luck. The shot above is of Dale Snodgrass in Excaliber, a Mustang owned by Jim Read with General Reg Urschler in Gunfighter as they fly out over lake Michigan during the Muskegon air show. The photo was again taken from the B-25 Lady Luck flown by Doug Weske and Patrick Harker.

This page clockwise from the top shows Brad Hood, Frank Borman and Lendy Renegar during the Oshkosh photo mission. Brad Hood is a 10,000 hour pilot with seat time in everything from the Aeronca Champ he first soloed at age 14 to the F-4 Phantom he flew while serving his country in the Air Force. This D model Mustang is owned by Charles Osborn and operated by Vintage Fighters which Brad now oversees down in Louisville, Kentucky. The next series of shots are from the backseat of Shangrila with Brad Hood at the controls. In the middle is a nice hero shot of Brad. On the lower left, you can see Eric Jachimowicz in the A-10 with Vlado Lenoch during a flight at the Indianapolis air show. The opposite page is during the same flight with Vlado in Moonbeam McSwine and Doogie in his custom painted personal Hog.

One of the true legendary pilots in the program, General Reg Urschler enlisted in the USAF in 1953. He attended basic training at Sampson AFB, NY and subsequently completed the Aviation Cadet program in 1955 when he was commissioned and awarded his pilot wings. Reg served 32 years on active duty primarily conducting Cold War reconnaissance missions against Communist Bloc countries. He has logged 13,000 flying hours, 1500 of which were in combat over Viet Nam. In 1985 he retired as Brigadier General. This shot of Reg in the CAF's P-51 Gunfighter was taken over Lake Winnebago during Oshkosh.

This page left is a variation shot of Lee Lauderback and Pinto Casey at Oceana. Top is General Reg Urschler on Gunfighter and the bottom shot is page is Vlado Lenoch in Moonbeam McSwine as he makes a formation takeoff with Brad Hood at Indianapolis. Vlado's great uncle was a Luftwaffe Ace with 36 victories in WWII.

This page is from Brad Hood's backseat in trail of Doogie in the A-10 and Vlado Lenoch at the Indianapolis air show. Opposite page clockwise from top is the Oshkosh mission again with Brad Hood, Frank Borman and Captain Lendy Renegar. The cockpit of Frank Borman's award winning TF-51. The Oceana flight with Lee Lauderback, Pinto Casey, and Doogie Jachimowicz. Frank Borman walking across the ramp for the afternoon Heritage Flight brief at Nellis. A variation of the Oceana echelon. A very clean trail stack of the flight out of Langley AFB with Jim Beasley, Ed Shipley, Dan Blue and Eric Jachimowicz.

This page clockwise from top is Lee Lauderback and Pinto Casey at Oceana, on the ground at with crew chief Angela West, a hero shot of Lee Lauderback and the national anthem being played at Nellis as the Golden Knights make the flag jump. Opposite page shows Snort Snodgrass doing his best PWAS smile for the camera in Jim Read's Mustang with Reg Urschler in close trail over Lake Michigan. Opposite top is a clean break over the lake while the shot below that is the main Heritage formation at Nellis AFB.

This page clockwise from top shows Frank Borman on the taxi back to the ramp after the Nellis Heritage Flight with Dale Snodgrass in the background. Bill Anders manning up at the Heritage Conference at Davis Monthan. Jimmy Beasley Jr. getting ready to go fly the lead at Langley. A great shot of the two Apollo 8 capsule mates as they get ready to go fly together one more time.

On the left is a great picture of general Bill Anders as he joins up over the Nevada desert behind Lady Luck with Col. frank Borman closing on his tail. The top shot here is a sharp looking formation takeoff of the two legends with the shot to the right showing them making a last minute review of the formation brief before taking off on the sunrise at Nellis AFB.

Major General William "Bill" Anders, call sign "Viking," is a retired Major General of the USAF Reserve with over 8000 hours of flying time. He was also a NASA astronaut and crew member with Frank Borman on the historic Apollo 8 mission to the Moon over Christmas of 1968. Apollo 8 was the first flight by mankind away from our home planet Earth to another body in our solar system. It was also the first manned flight of the Saturn V rocket. During their 10 orbits of the Moon the three man crew including Jim Lovell read the first few verses from the book of Genesis and Bill took the famous "Earthrise" photograph that landed on the cover of LIFE Magazine.

It has been a special honor to fly with these men.

This page shows all images of Chuck Hall in his P-51 with Captain Scott Shephard in the F-16 from Hill AFB during the initial photo mission shot from the EC-130 of the 43rd ECS at Davis-Monthan. The lower right shot was made by Col. Michael Hoyes from the backseat of Chuck's Mustang while in trail behind the Herc. Chuck is based in southern California and has raced at Reno in years past.

The shot of the left was taken at Langley with Jim Beasley Jr. in lead of Ed Shipley, Dan Blue and Eric Jachimowicz. The shot above is Major Dean "Wilbur" Wright on the left with Ed Shipley on the right during the Langley AFB air show. Wilbur is a former lead solo with the Thunderbirds and has flown A-10s, F-16s, F-117s and the British Harrier during two exchange tours to the UK. It was during those exchange duties that he met and married his wife Andrea Storer of York, UK, a former RAF Flt Lt.

The shot on the lower right is of Reg Urschler in Gunfighter, Tom Gregory in the Lone Star Museum's P-47 Thunderbolt Tar Healed Hal and Major John York in the F-15 Eagle during a flight at Oshkosh.

F-86 SABRE JET

As America's first swept wing fighter, the F-86 Sabre was also the first production aircraft to reach supersonic speeds going downhill. In the skies over Korea, she earned the handle "MiG Master" scoring a 14:1 kill ratio and producing 39 aces. These days, Dale Snodgrass and Ed Shipley offer breathtaking demonsrations that showcase the Sabre's grace and speed.

Ed Shipley leads Major Dan Blue out over the eastern shore of Maryland. The F-86 Sabre that Ed owns and flies was previously owned by Frank Borman who restored the airplane as an exact replica of the jet he flew while based at Luke AFB. Photo ship: C-130H of the 143rd AW.

In December 1950 production began on the F-86E. This version featured a revised control system which incorporated an all-flying tail with linked elevators, power boosting for the tail controls and artificial "feel" for all control surfaces. The USAF accepted 333 -E models, all powered by the same J47-GE-13 engine as the -A model.

Pressures exerted by and lessons learned during the Korean War led to the opening of a second Sabre construction line in Columbus, OH, to produce the F-86F. This version incorporated a new wing leading edge. It was extended 6 in at the root and 3 in at the tip, the slats were eliminated and the wings were fitted with small boundary fences.

An engine change was also done with the 5,970 lb s.t. J47-GE-27 being fitted. These changes led to a subsequent increase in performance with top speed being increased by 15 mph to 690. Rate of climb was increased from 7,630 ft/min to 10,000 ft/min with range being increased from 785 mi to 1,270 mi. Armament remained unchanged. Two thousand five hundred forty F-86Fs were built with the

last being delivered in December 1956.

The F-86H was the last production version of the Sabre to be accepted by the USAF and incorporated many new changes. It had a 2 in increase in wingspan, the fuselage was lengthened by 14 in, a larger tailplane without dihedral was added, and heavier landing gear was installed.

An armament change was also made with 4 20-mm cannon replacing the 6 0.50s in the nose. It was powered by the J73-GE-3E engine which produced 8,920 lb s.t. Performance again improved with a top speed of 692 mph and a rate of climb of 12,900 ft/min. Range decreased, however, to 1,040 mi, a difference of 230 mi from the -F. North American produced 473 -H models before production ceased in August 1955.

The final large-scale production model of the Sabre was the F-86D or "Sabre Dog." Designed as an all-weather interceptor, production of this version, which began in March 1951, finally totaled 2,504 aircraft. Originally designated as the YF-95A, the Sabre Dog incorporated a number of de-

sign changes which altered both its performance and its appearance. The nose was re-contoured to carry radar above the intake, the fuselage was wider and length increased by almost 3 in. Armament changes were also made. The guns were deleted in favor of a retractable tray housing 24 2.75 in rockets.

Power was provided by a J47-GE-17 engine with afterburner which produced 5,700 and 7,630 lb s.t. respectively. With the afterburner rate of climb increased to 17,800 ft/min and a slight increase in top speed to 707 mph was achieved. Range dropped dramatically, however, to only 836 mi, only slightly more than the original -A model.

The Sabre was not America's first jet fighter but to many pilots it was the first to win both their respect and their hearts. Compared to today's fighters it is underpowered and primitive but few aircraft have done so well at the job they were designed to do. With their classic good looks the F-86 Sabre was the right aircraft at the right time and earned itself a prominent place in aviation history.

-Jim Muche

Left: Dale Snodgrass tucks the F-86 in behind the C-130 while making turns over Newport, Rhode Island. This page: Captain Eric Jachimowicz in the A-10 follows the F-86 in trail during the same mission over Newport.

Clockwise from Top: Dale Snodgrass makes his trademark photo pass for the crowd at Hanscom AFB, another look at the Sabre from the ramp of the C-130J, Snort talks to the airboss after startup in the cockpit, Snort and his crew team for the F-86, father and son duo Mike Dannels and Larry Leaf hide out under the wing for some shade during the show at Quonset Point, Rhode Island. Opposite page shows a single ship image of the F-86 over Newport.

Ed Shipley and Major Dan Blue execute a crossover break during a photo flight out of Langley AFB. Opposite page shows the same two guys in a variation of the formation flown behind the C-130. Ed Shipley is seen in the far top image in the cockpit of his F-86 during the Langley show in Virginia.

Above: Backlit by a setting sun over the Chesapeake bay, Ed Shipley leads Major Dan Blue back to Langley after the photo flight profile is complete. Opposite page depicts Dale Snodgrass in a low flat pass during the Oceana airshow. Left to right below that is Snort walking with Dan McCue, a longtime friend of the Heritage Flight program. The cockpit of Snort's F-86 and the tailgate briefing session for the dual Heritage Flight formations during the Nellis show. Visible are pilots Frank Borman, Dale Snodgrass, Bill Anders, Steve Hinton, Lendy Renegar, Tom Gregory and the back of Robert Kiebler.

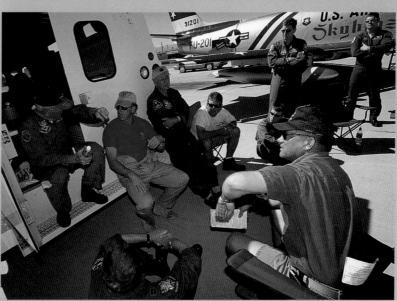

During one of the more dramatic photo missions of this entire project, the flight out of Nellis AFB was the grand finale as far as dissimilar formation flying is concerned. In a single flight we photographed nine different aircraft types from the tail gunner position of Lady Luck, the B-25 flown by Doug Weske and Patrick Harker. The image above shows Dale Snodgrass leading a glorious "vic" with Steve Hinton in the P-38, Tom Gregory in the P-47, and both Frank Borman and Bill Anders in their Mustangs. Captain Scott Shepard is seen pulling out of the formation from the safety observer position. Opposite page show variations on the theme with Lendy Renegar taking the safety role in the F-15. Top image is Snort and Alamo on roll-out after returning from their Heritage demo at Nellis.